Wearable Warriors
Women Driving the Fashion Tech Movement

Gwendolyn Theresa Jackson

Table of Contents

The advance of technology is based on making it fit in so that you don't really even notice it, so it's part of everyday life.

Chapter 1. Introduction

Unveiling a remarkable fusion of technology and fashion, our Special Report titled "Wearable Warriors: Women Driving the Fashion Tech Movement" moves beyond catwalks and boutiques, guiding you into a progressive realm where cutting-edge innovation meets timeless style. In an exciting revelation, our work outlines the tenacity and creativity of several pioneering women dynamizing this transformative industry. Their brilliant exploits have not only given wings to futuristic wearable designs but also ignited a revolutionary change in the global fashion conscience. If you have an appetite for captivating stories, radical new concepts, and a desire to ride this exciting wave of fashion technology, this special report is an absolute must-buy! Hold your breath and prepare to step into a world where style isn't just what you wear but also how innovatively you wear it!

Chapter 2. Bridging the Chasm: Where Technology Meets Fashion

The fusion of fashion and technology initiates a paradigm shift, rewriting the rules and rendering the erstwhile dichotomy moot. No longer existing in separate silos, they've eagerly converged at a crossroads, creating a dynamic industry that marries style with innovation, tradition with futurism.

2.1. The Emergence of Fashion Tech

The dawn of fashion tech was neither a grand eureka moment nor a disruption. Instead, it was more of a gradual, harmonious confluence, born from the mutual and innate desire for progression inherent to both fashion and technology sectors. The fashion industry, known for its continuous quest for novelty and individuality, recognized the limitless possibilities technology held to bring in hitherto unimagined design processes, materials, and wearability, thereby redefining the meaning of style and the very way we dress. On the other hand, technology, in its constant strive to permeate all aspects of human life, found in fashion a fertile ground for its spread and an unmatched avenue for making tangible its often-intangible ideas.

Early adapters were brave pioneers, like Hussein Chalayan, who wowed the audiences with dresses that morphed their shape and style on the runway using microcontrollers and servo motors. There was no turning back since then. The stage was set for an industry that was as chic as it was smart. The chasm was bridging; fashion and technology were meeting at last.

2.2. Quantum Leaps in Wearable Tech

The harmonizing of fashion and technology sparked the advent of wearable tech, a genre that left behind the clunky devices strapped on arms or pockets. Wearable tech brought forth elegant applications integrating seamlessly into daily apparel, almost invisible to the naked eye, complementing style while offering utility.

Be it fitness trackers that double as sleek bracelets, smartwatches that echo high-street fashion trends, or jackets with in-built heating elements tailor-made for inclement weather, wearable technology was no longer just about convenience; it was also about making strong fashion statements. The weave of tech threads into fabrics did not bind the wearer but, on the contrary, freed them from the shackles of regularly held sand-timers, sun-dials, pocket watches, mobile devices, and more.

2.3. New Avenues in Textiles

What stood out in this amalgamation was how technology altered the very materiality of fashion – the textiles. Smart fabrics turned the tables, whole bearable technology interweaving into the warp and weft of the textiles themselves. Whether it was photochromic inks changing color under sunlight, thermoreactive threads altering patterns with body heat, or conductive yarns acting as touch screen compatible surfaces, technology began to redefine the possibilities of what fabrics could do.

These futuristic textiles are the foundation of the nascent field of 'soft circuits' or 'e-textiles', where electronics are embedded directly into fabrics. Garments with integrated sensors to monitor body temperature, heart-rate, or other health metrics are no longer a distant dream. The weave of electronic components and conductive threads will ensure seamless integration that negates any discomfort for the wearer.

2.4. Fashion Tech and Sustainability

This marriage between fashion and technology also holds promises for a sustainable future. Tech-enabled recycling, efficient manufacturing through automated systems and AI, and the use of biotech to produce eco-friendly textiles are just some instances of how this integration can lead to a more sustainable fashion ecosystem.

Furthermore, smart clothes can have a longer lifespan as technology enables garments to transform and adapt as per changing needs. Whether it's self-cleaning fabrics that reduce water waste or clothing that alters shapes to fit over time, the innovations in this sector promise a reduction in fashion waste and subsequently, a move towards sustainability.

As we wrap up this chapter, it becomes clear that the merging of technology and fashion is less about bridging a chasm and more about weaving an intricate tapestry together. This is a story of symbiosis and synergy, where technology enhances the artistry, functionality and sustainability of fashion, and fashion gives technology a tactile, visually appealing outlet to express itself. In the subsequent chapters, we will delve deeper into this fascinating interface, mapping the journey, analyzing trends, and predicting the exciting pathway that lies ahead in the Fashion Tech landscape.

Chapter 3. The Pioneering Women Trailblazing the Fashion Tech Frontier

To embark on this intricate journey of innovation, ingenuity, and inspiration, we commence by illuminating the remarkable narratives of the pioneering women who are setting the pace in the fashion tech frontier. Their passion is to transform and mold the industry into a harmonious marriage of aesthetics and technology, birthing a realm where fashion does not just beautify, but also empowers, equips, and enlightens.

3.1. Birth of the Movement: A Technological Renaissance

In the early stages, fashion and technology seemed like distant worlds. The amalgamation of the two was like oil and water; they appeared incompatible. However, women with indomitable spirits, unyielding determination, and a visionary spark decided not just to bridge this gap, but to transcend it. This gave birth to the marriage of fashion and technology, creating unparalleled revolutions.

Leading this transformation was a group of pioneering women whose names are now etched indelibly into the annals of fashion tech history. They dared to break free from the traditional, envisioning wearable technology that resonated with style, femininity, and practicality, while shedding the commonplace perception of 'tech for tech's sake'.

3.2. Fashion Tech Visionaries: The Radical Women Trio

Three trailblazers who've significantly contributed to the evolution of fashion tech are Elizabeth Rossiello, Pinaclara Morano, and Joséphine Goube. Their pioneering explorations have become archetypes for successive trailblazers to follow.

Elizabeth Rossiello forged a path in digital payment systems through her startup BitPesa. Integrating blockchain technology, BitPesa revolutionized the financial handling within the fashion industry, introducing efficiency, accountability, and transparency in transactions. This revolutionary approach meant the supply chain processes became smoother, faster, more cost-effective, and thus propelled the industry into the digital era.

Contrasting Rossiello's sphere of impact, Pinaclara Morano targeted the textile side of fashion tech. Morano's company, BioShades, combined bioengineering and digital fabrication to produce sustainable, eco-friendly textiles. Using a home-grown process that integrated biology with innovative techniques, BioShades offered an array of fabrics that were not only trend-setting but were also contributing towards a greener future.

The third visionary, Joséphine Goube, looked at fashion tech from a unique socio-political perspective. As CEO of TechFugees, Goube propagated the use of wearable tech to aid refugees, transforming wearable fashion gadgets into tools of empowerment, engagement, and safety for marginalized communities.

3.3. Broadening Horizons: Onwards to Mass Market

After these individual success stories, the aim was to broaden the consumer base. Making wearable tech accessible, appealing, and practical for the masses became the new goal. Trendsetters such as Lucy Beard, founder and CEO of Feetz - a 3D printing shoe company, revolutionized the shoe industry by personalizing every customer's experience, providing both comfort and style in a sustainable manner. This venture is just one example of how women in the fashion tech industry are creating consumer-oriented solutions, taking the market by storm.

Another significant contributor to this expansion was Melissa Koole, founder of FashNerd. She introduced the concept of smart textiles into fashion tech, proposing novel innovations that transformed everyday clothing from just attire to technological companions.

3.4. The Continuing Journey: Future Trailblazers

Our exploration of trailblazers would be unjust without casting an eye towards the future. Young, aspiring leaders like Jennifer Chong, co-founder of Linjer, are continually pushing the envelope. Chong's groundbreaking approach to luxury fashion with sustainability at its core pointed towards the future of the industry. Moreover, entrepreneurs like Ashwini Srikantiah, the mind behind Qatch- a personalized shopping service targetting social media, further exemplify how tireless innovation and creativity will continually redefine the fashion tech landscape.

The journey through the multifaceted terrain of the fashion-tech movement is a testament to the pioneering spirit of these relentless warriors. Their ventures have not only changed the outlook on what fashion can accomplish but laid the blueprints for aspiring entrepreneurs and innovators worldwide. Their dreams nurturing capabilities of utilitarian fashion tech are a reminder to us, as readers and consumers - innovation is limitless. Our fashion, our technology, our impact - in the end, it all boils down to our imagination. Bigger the dreams, greater the revolutions.

Chapter 4. Innovative Applications in Wearable Fashion Tech

Beyond thresholds and bastions universally acknowledged, in the realm where technology graces fashion, we encounter scintillating marvels of wearable fashion tech. With ceaseless edification of technology swirling its plea in a sartorial gathering, one is left to wonder about the cardinal pioneering genres that have ushered in this era of wearable tech.

4.1. Innovative Wearable Tech: A General Overview

Wearable technology as a standalone concept isn't a novice entrant in the technological panorama. From smartwatches that seamlessly consolidate the functionalities of a phone, a sports band, and a watch, to health trackers recording various data points, the realm of wearable tech has been consistently expanding. However, the real revelation lies in the marriage of this technology with the art of fashion. Coupling vogue with utility, innovation marries style; the demonstration of such matrimony is what we'll journey into in this segment.

4.2. Smart Clothing: A Leap into the Future

Imagine a world where your apparel does much more than merely clothe you. Welcome to the world of smart clothing - a realm where garments come with embedded sensors, chips, and conductive threads, allowing an interactive experience.

Smart clothing takes a number of innovative forms. Various fashion-tech pioneers have tinkered with thermochromic dyes that change color with varying body temperatures, thereby making clothing an intuitive reflection of one's internal physical state. On the other hand, sports gear is being elevated with inbuilt GPS systems for navigational purposes and haptic feedback mechanisms to provide athletes with real-time physical feedback on their performance.

Constituting the apex of smart clothing innovation is the concept of bio-monitoring garments. We are edging closer to a reality where sophisticated pieces of clothing like smart bras and intelligent shirts monitor our vital bodily metrics, such as heart rate, blood pressure, and body temperature, and relay this information to medical professionals.

4.3. Fashionable Wearable Tech Devices: When Style Meets Function

The accessories we traditionally wear have also been bolstered with the power of tech. Innovations in jewellery, watches, glasses, and even shoes have crossed the chasm between style and function. Now, a ring is not just a piece of jewellery, but also a sleep monitor or a fitness tracker. Similarly, glasses come equipped with augmented reality displays and interactive capabilities. Shoes have evolved from simple foot gear to intelligent moving machines that cater to various conditions and applications such as elderly assistance, posture correction, and performance enhancement.

One cannot overlook the rise of smartwatches and fitness bands that emulate the chic of a trendy bracelet and the utility of a personal computer, all in a single package. These accessories monitor our vitals, keep us connected with the digital world, and even serve as standalone multimedia devices.

4.4. Intelligent Textiles: Threads that Speak

In the cradle of technological innovation, textiles have been revolutionized. Known as e-textiles, these futuristic materials seamlessly amalgamate the realms of textiles and electronic components.

From fabrics altering their properties based on weather conditions to textiles illuminating with embedded LEDs, the landscape of e-textiles is both riveting and continuously evolving. Another exciting facet is kinetic energy harvesting fabrics that harness the energy imparted to them during movements and convert it into electrical energy - a promising frontier for wearable tech.

Integrative textile technology is permeating various sectors, with applications becoming apparent in fields as varied as health monitoring (think smart bandages), fashion, space exploration, and more.

As we elucidate these innovative applications in wearable fashion tech, one cannot help but appreciate the ingenious human mind that continues to defy constraints and redefine norms. However, these advancements also pave way for an array of challenges that need careful analysis and clever strategies for mitigation. As we witnessthe ceaseless blending of technology and sartorial art in myriad ways, we look forward to a future adorned with the elegance of style and the might of tech. The exploration of this enthralling space continues, teasing us with untapped possibilities just waiting to be discovered.

So, as we advance, let's keep looking into the future with curiosity and wonder, for in the world of fashion tech, the adage holds true: the only constant thing is change. This is merely the commencement of an epoch that promises to redefine our outlook and challenge our preconceptions, as we evolve with the fabric of time, bearing witness to the revolution of wearable tech in fashion.

Chapter 5. Breakthroughs in Fabric: Materials that Redefine Boundaries

As we embark on the fascinating journey of fabric evolution, it is imperative to first acknowledge the longstanding foundation that traditional textiles have provided for centuries. Cotton, silk, wool, and linen - these materials have graced our wardrobes for generations, shaping the aesthetics and functionality of garments throughout history. However, as we stand at the precipice of the 21st century, it's clear that the demand for more adaptable, sustainable and technologically advanced materials asks us to push beyond these textile traditions. This era signals the advent of breakthroughs in fabrics, materials that are redefining boundaries and changing the shape of the fashion industry, an exploration that this chapter will unpack meticulously.

5.1. The Genesis of Smart Fabrics

At the onset of the 21st century, the concept of 'smart fabrics' emerged, throwing light on a whole universe of previously unimagined possibilities. Smart fabrics, also known as e-textiles, are the amalgamation of electronics and textiles, which have the ability to interact with their environment and the user. From simple color changes in response to temperature fluctuations to biofeedback-sensing clothing, smart fabrics have started to redefine the boundaries of conventional textiles. The pioneers in this field have, over the years, worked relentlessly on breakthrough fabric technologies to make smart fabrics a reality.

5.2. Revolution of Fabrics through Nanotechnology

The advent of nanotechnology in the textile industry signified another milestone in fabric breakthroughs. The science of manipulating particles at a nanoscale, roughly 100,000 times smaller than the width of a human hair, opened up new horizons for textile functionality. This resulted in fabrics with superior qualities- stain resistance, wrinkle-free, anti-odor, UV protection, and even self-cleaning properties. Commendable in regard to this advancement is the fact that these benefits were achieved without compromising the tactile feel, breathability, or aesthetics of the fabric; instead, they enhanced the user's comfort level while blending seamlessly with the fabric's essential look and function.

5.3. Bioengineered Fabrics: The Rise of Lab-Grown Materials

The rise of bioengineered fabrics added a whole new dimension to the materials available to the fashion industry. Pioneering companies have developed ways to grow leather in labs without harming animals, thus providing an eco-friendly alternative to traditional leather production. Spider silk, bio-engineered cotton, mushroom-derived materials - the realm of bioengineered fabrics has seen an explosion in recent years. These materials are designed keeping sustainability and ethical considerations at the forefront, making them an exciting area of growth with significant potential for fashion's future.

5.4. Conductive Textiles: Electricity on the Go

Perhaps one of the most fascinating integrations we have seen in the textile industry is the development of conductive textiles. Woven with a combination of traditional and conductive threads, these fabrics can transmit electricity, data, and even heat, opening up an entirely new realm of wearable electronics. From light-up dresses to touch-sensitive clothing, conductive textiles have unlocked a new level of interactive expression.

5.5. Wearable Solar: Harnessing Power

Lastly, wearable solar fabrics deserve a special mention owing to their innovative confluence of fashion, technology, and sustainability. Imbued with thin-film solar cells, these fabrics can harness sunlight and convert it into electricity, making it feasible to power small electronics directly from one's clothing. This innovation marks a significant step toward renewable energy and sustainable fashion practices.

5.6. The Challenges and the Road Ahead

While these advancements hold monumental promise, the integration of novel materials into the mainstream fashion industry is fraught with challenges. As fashion tech continues to evolve, scalability, affordability, washability, and user comfort will be defining factors in the transformation of these innovative fabric technologies from science fiction to everyday reality. The future of fashion lies not only in the advancement of these technologies, but also in their successful implementation, addressing social, environmental, and ethical concerns, thereby truly revolutionizing the canvas of fabric technology.

As we wind up our expedition into the world of breakthrough fabrics, it becomes clear that the future of the fashion-tech industry will not just be about smart devices and gadgets, but also about smart fabrics that are woven with ingenious technology, profound perception, and considerable anticipation for future requirements. These new materials are more than just textiles; they are an amalgamation of science, technology, fashion and sustainability. The boundaries they are pushing are not merely physical dimensions, but the very definition of what fabric can be and can achieve. As these breakthroughs in fabric continue to gain momentum, we are truly standing at the crossroads of fashion annals, anticipating the onset of an epoch where our very clothes will be a testament to innovation, adaptability and sustainable design. Beyond every thread and fiber, the future of fabrics holds an exciting and infinite potential that is sure to redefine the landscape of fashion as we know it. Perhaps, our clothes will not just be things we wear, but entities that we interact with, and extensions of our very identities.

Chapter 6. Revolutions in Design: Aesthetics in the Era of Tech

The industrial revolution in the eighteenth and nineteenth centuries rendered a profound impact by altering the landscape of design, forever shattering the conventional norms of aesthetics. In the same way, the current influx of technology in the industry is also reshaping the contours of design dramatically. This era has seen a paradigm shift from traditional design strategies to a new-age amalgamation of technology and aesthetics, leading to unprecedented transformations that stretch the boundaries of what is possible.

6.1. Paradigm Shift: From Traditional to Technological Aesthetics

Traditionally, every stitch and seam in a garment formed under the designer's watchful eye, complying with their artistic vision. However, with innovations like 3D printing, sophisticated design software, artificial intelligence, and augmented reality, the art of fashion is swiftly adopting a high-tech perspective. Designers no longer limit themselves to mere visualization; they now model designs in three dimensions, study physics and environmental dynamics, and conduct multiple iterations before the physical prototype comes into being.

Concurrently, artificial intelligence has played a pivotal role in this shift. AI has taken over regular tasks such as pattern drafting and resizing, saving time for the designers and allowing their creative energy to flow, unhampered. Furthermore, AI has facilitated a holistic analysis of customers' preferences and fashion trends, assisting design decisions more accurately than human intuition alone.

6.2. Reimagining Fashion with Augmented and Virtual Reality

Augmented and Virtual Reality technologies have introduced an entirely new dimension to the fashion design process. They provide a digital space where objects can be manipulated, adjusted, and observed from different angles without the need for a physical prototype. By utilizing these technologies, trial and error become notably less time-consuming and costly, allowing designers to experiment more freely.

Moreover, VR and AR imbue the design process with a degree of interactivity previously unattainable. Concepts and designs can be examined and modified in real-time, leading to instant feedback and faster design iterations.

6.3. 3D Printing: Crafting the Future of Fashion

When it comes to revolutionary design techniques, 3D printing holds a vanguard position. It has the potential to completely overturn traditional conventions of clothing production by enabling the creation of clothing from virtually any material. With this cutting-edge technology, designers can infuse intricate detailing, striking structures, and innovative textures in their designs without the constraints imposed by weaving, cutting, and stitching traditional fabrics.

Further expanding the realm of possibilities, 3D printed clothing can also carry embedded technology. This could include sensors to track health data, built-in climate control features, or electroluminescent panels that change the garment's color based on the wearer's mood or environment.

6.4. Sustainable Designs: A Technological Triumph

Beyond revolutionizing aesthetics and design processes, technology has also paved the path towards sustainability in fashion. New materials derived from algae, coffee, pineapple, and other organic substances, combined with innovative textile engineering techniques, promise an eco-friendlier future for fashion.

Additionally, advanced processing technology and innovative dyeing techniques significantly reduce raw material wastage and water pollution associated with traditional methods. By propagating the use of biotechnology, recycled materials, and non-toxic dyes, technology has set the stage for sustainable and aesthetically pleasing fashion choices.

6.5. Biomimicry: Harnessing Nature's Aesthetics

Last but not least, biomimicry - the practice of emulating nature's patterns and strategies - has gained momentum in the fashion tech landscape. Nature, with its impeccable design techniques honed over millennia, has become an abundant repository of inspiration.

Through advanced technologies, designers can now replicate the intricate patterns found in nature, or mimic the properties of a certain plant or animal, to create designs that are not only visually stunning but also highly functional. For instance, fabrics infused with properties emulating a lotus leaf's self-cleaning attribute or clothing that changes colour like a chameleon. Biomimicry is bridging the gap between fashion and nature, proving that design, technology, and nature can coexist harmoniously.

As we step into a future replete with countless technological marvels, it is clear that the symbiosis of aesthetics and technology will continue to revolutionize fashion design. The narrative woven in the pages of this chapter revolves around this radical transition, illuminating the breakthroughs that are reshaping our understanding of design and aesthetics in the era of technology. Hopefully, the insights shared here will not only act as a catalyst for thought but also inspire more groundbreaking innovations in the vibrant world of fashion technology.

Chapter 7. Fashion Sustainability: Technological Solutions to Age-Old Problems

The narrative now unfolds in the verdant field of fashion sustainability, an area that's rapidly gaining momentum in a world grappling with the specter of environmental damage. Technological advancements have a significant role to play, capable of proffering solutions to an array of long-standing problems.

7.1. The Issue of Fast Fashion

One of the most pervasive challenges is 'fast fashion,' a term used to describe inexpensive clothing that rapidly replicates high fashion trends. While it seemingly enables the democratization of fashion, it carries grave environmental implications. Clothes are worn and discarded at an alarming rate, leading to vast amounts of waste, while factories churn out these goods, often in unregulated conditions, spewing pollutants into the air and water.

Over the past decades, with the advent of globalization and e-commerce, this issue has skyrocketed. The sheer volume of fashion waste generated worldwide is staggering: an estimated annual figure of 92 million tons, according to a report from the Ellen MacArthur Foundation.

7.2. Innovative Technologies for a Circular Fashion Industry

Comprehending this dilemma, many pioneering women in the fashion tech industry have turned to innovative technological solutions to tackle the environmental impact of the fashion industry, at all stages of the lifecycle of garments, promoting a more circular economy.

These innovators harness technologies like blockchain to increase transparency and traceability, ensuring that brands and consumers can make informed choices about materials and production chains. Products made through sustainable processes, using eco-friendly materials, can be certified and traced using blockchain technology. Moreover, technologies such as artificial intelligence and machine learning can predict trends, reduce overproduction, and manage inventory more efficiently.

7.3. Integrating Tech in Fabric Waste Management

Another remarkable example is integrating technology in managing fabric waste. Advanced technologies are being deployed to recycle, repurpose, or compost old clothing, turning waste into resource. Physical recycling techniques, like mechanical and chemical recycling, are combined with smart technologies. For instance, textiles embedded with radio-frequency identification (RFID) or near-field communication (NFC) can improve sorting and recycling processes.

Some companies are pioneering producing clothing from repurposed materials, using tech-enabled processes. Companies like "Renewcell" transform discarded cotton into "Circulose," a new type of material that looks and feels like virgin quality, but with significantly lesser environmental impact.

7.4. The Emergence of Smart and Sustainable Materials

Simultaneously, technological breakthroughs in the field of materials science have given rise to 'smart and sustainable materials.' Biofabrication, the use of living organisms to create products, is making its mark in the fashion industry. Companies like 'Bolt Threads' are harnessing yeast and bacteria to create spider silk and mushroom leather, providing sustainable alternatives to traditional, high-impact materials.

Additionally, nanotechnologies are being applied to improve the functionality of fabrics, making them more durable, thereby reducing the need for replacements and promoting sustainability.

7.5. The Promising Future of Tech-Driven Sustainability

Technology has just started revolutionizing the fashion industry's impact on the environment. Its potential is vast, and the myriad of technological interventions in consideration and in practice is remarkable. From AI-driven demand forecasting, reducing overproduction, to biofabricated materials replacing traditional, environmentally harmful ones, we're witness to an evolving narrative of a greener, sustainable future for the fashion industry.

However, four key elements must converge to ensure the successful integration of technology and sustainability in fashion: governmental regulations ensuring sustainable practices, investor support, consumer awareness, and industry-wide collaboration.

In the ensuing chapters, we delve deeper into the world of fashion tech startups, the emerging consumer trends, and the challenges that still need addressing. With each word, we aim to stir the curiosity of fashion enthusiasts, technology aficionados, and conscious consumers to explore and engage in this exciting, dynamic intersection of fashion and technology. Our journey underscores the instrumental role women play, as we navigate the burgeoning landscape of fashion tech, gleaning insights into the economic, environmental, and social potential it holds.

Indeed, technology-driven sustainability in fashion is not just a solution to age-old problems. It is a bold, futuristic envisioning of a world where style, innovation and care for the planet harmoniously intertwine.

Chapter 8. Consumer Trends in Fashion Tech: A Peek into the Future

As a curious observer from the periphery, trying to decode the complex lacework of fashion technology, one may feel somewhat perplexed. However, delving deep into this terrain and scrutinizing it under a microscope, one can identify certain marked trends that are not only shaping the industry as a whole but also molding consumer preferences and behavior.

8.1. The Reign of Personalization

The epoch of personalization has arrived in the fashion industry, leveraging technology to offer a strikingly tailored experience to each consumer. With the advent of AI-driven algorithms, custom-fit clothing is now attainable on a mass scale. These digital tools deployed within e-commerce platforms take into account a myriad of individual measurements and preferences, manufacturing clothing that fits as if it were designed exclusively for the wearer. This level of customization has significantly influenced consumer purchasing behavior in fashion, tilting the scales towards a more personal approach to fashion tech.

8.2. Sustainability as a Prerogative

Environmental consciousness has been growing among consumers, setting the stage for sustainable fashion technologies to enter the mainstream. This trend isn't just pushing the boundaries of eco-friendly materials but also influencing the entire garment lifecycle. Innovative startups are supplementing this growing trend with developments such as bio-fabrics and recycling technologies. These advancements in technology offer clothing ranges that are not only stylish, but also sustainable. Consumers have shown a burgeoning inclination towards these eco-friendly options, catalyzing a dynamic shift in buying trends.

8.3. The Rise of Smart Clothing

With the proliferation of fitness-centered technology such as fitness trackers and running gear, smart clothing is becoming a part of the everyday wardrobe. These garments offer an amalgamation of fashion and tech, retaining aesthetic appeal while integrating sensors or other elements that track biometric data, enhancing convenience for the user. The emergence of this subsector is reshaping consumer behavior in fashion, edging towards a preference for functionality intertwined with aesthetics.

8.4. The Ascendancy of Virtual and Augmented Reality

The use of Virtual Reality (VR) and Augmented Reality (AR) in the fashion industry has opened a platonic Pandora's box, offering consumers the ability to virtually try-on clothes, even before making a purchase. The ability to visualize and digitally manipulate an outfit according to the consumer's preferences offers a retail experience unlike any other. This trend is shifting consumer choices towards online platforms which offer such immersive shopping experiences.

8.5. The Shift Towards Direct-to-Consumer Brands

Technology advancements, along with a desire for a more direct connection with consumers, have paved way for a significant rise in direct-to-consumer brands. This approach allows brands to provide consumers with high-quality products at competitive prices by eliminating the middlemen. Consumers are readily embracing these brands, further initiating a meaningful shift in the retail landscape.

This comprehensive look at each of the trends at the frontier of fashion technology brings into sharp relief the role of innovative women in driving this evolution. Propelled by their relentless efforts and unwavering vision, the confluence of style and technology is pushing boundaries, gradually transforming the fashion ethos across the globe.

However, forecasting future consumer trends in the fashion tech industry isn't so straightforward. Rapid advancements in technology and the ever-evolving consumer preferences compound this complexity. Nonetheless, with anticipation, we can look towards a future where digital fabrics, AI-driven personal shopping assistants, fabric recycling on the micro-scale, and eco-conscious manufacturing processes become the norm rather than the exception. Indeed, a world where technological innovation is not just adorning the fashion scene but vivifying it in all its glory!

This voyage into forecasting and analyzing intelligible consumer insights in the fashion tech industry brings to the fore the paradigm shifts that are debilitating the traditional models of outfits and attire. It is only through a vantage point of understanding and appreciating these changes, can one truly comprehend the magnitude and momentum the fashion tech industry holds. As fashion tech trends continue to evolve and amalgamate with consumer behavior, we find ourselves at a unique precipice, one which leads to an exciting, tech-integrated vista of style and substance.

Chapter 9. Fashion Tech Startups: Breeding Ground for Innovation

In the world of fashion, the role of technology cannot be underestimated. The synergy between these two sectors has given birth to innovations that are rapidly transforming the industry. Fashion and technology are seamlessly blending in ways that spell out a burgeoning new era. Fast-growing fashion tech startups are leading the charge, pushing boundaries and enabling fashion to evolve at an unprecedented pace. This space serves as a breeding ground for new ideas, bringing forth revolutionary innovations that define this progressive landscape.

9.1. The Rise of Fashion Tech Startups

Fashion tech startups occupy a unique niche at the intersection of fashion and technology, leveraging modern techniques to create, distribute, and market fashionable clothing and accessories. Their trajectory has soared considerably with the advent of smart fabrics and wearable technology, coupled with the growing awareness for sustainable fashion and the rise in e-commerce.

Fashion technology startups are not confined to mere product innovation. They encapsulate a broader spectrum, facilitating digital transformations through virtual fitting rooms, AI-powered fashion designing, blockchain-enabled supply chain transparency, machine learning for trend forecasting, and ecommerce platforms.

Many of these startups are fueled by a rising class of women entrepreneurs who are bravely venturing into the tech space, bringing a fresh, creative perspective. They are addressing market gaps, enhancing user experiences, and transforming the fashion world as we know it. Their endeavours resonate powerfully, demonstrating that fervent creativity, when combined with technological savvy, can engineer profound changes.

9.2. Pioneering Startups and Their Innovative Models

Numerous startups are forging ahead, despite challenges, with innovative business models and products. Zilingo, a Singapore-based unicorn, explores the B2B fashion space, helping businesses digitise, while providing sourcing, financing, and marketing solutions. Stitch Fix revolutionizes online shopping with AI-powered personalized styling services; they combine artificial intelligence with human intuition to curate customized fashion boxes for their customers.

Unmade, a London-based startup, has introduced an innovative business model by offering bespoke knitwear. Their on-demand production platform allows consumers to customize their garments, illustrating how customization can help businesses reduce waste and embrace sustainability.

In the smart clothing arena, Wearable X stands out as an inspiring startup. They blend fashion and technology to create apparel with "embedded tech", such as their NadiX yoga pants, enabled with haptic technology for real-time feedback on yoga poses.

These startups are just a few instances from a vibrant ecosystem that continually brims with new ideas, reshaping the fashion landscape.

9.3. Sustaining Success: Navigating Challenges and Roadblocks

While the runway to the future is promising, the flight isn't turbulence-free. Fashion tech has its share of roadblocks. One prominent challenge is funding. While tech startups can often find venture capital firms eager to invest, fashion tech startups face more skepticism due to perceived risk and complexity.

Additionally, consumer acceptance of new technologies can be slow, requiring substantial marketing efforts. Other hurdles may involve material sourcing, sustainability concerns, technological integration, or even regulatory challenges. However, the spirit of entrepreneurship thrives on overcoming obstacles, and numerous success stories attest to this spirit of resilience.

9.4. Creating a Future Ready Fashion World

It is thrilling to observe the fashion tech startup landscape evolve, playing a defining role in reimagining our sartorial future. The industry's next phase will undoubtedly see the rise of many more exciting startups pushing the envelope, while positively impacting societal norms and environmental footprint.

In a world where technology is increasingly permeating every walk of life, these startups are steadfast in their mission to lead the future of fashion. Their innovative ideas signify an era where style, sustainability, and technology come together, to forever change our wardrobe narratives. This exciting paradigm shift, led by fashion tech startups, is ushering us into a future where the apparel we wear says much more about us than simply a fashion statement. It begins to narrate the story of our evolving relationship with technology, and our growing consciousness towards sustainability.

Fashion and technology, once seen as disparate worlds, are now knitting together a new era, and it's the fashion tech startups that hold the needles. They are the true breeding ground for innovation, daring to challenge the status quo and rewrite the rules of a time-honoured industry. Their courage and creativity fuel a change that's nothing short of revolutionary. One thing's for sure - as these startups continue to thrive, we'll witness even more dramatic transformations, with the world of fashion at the forefront of this remarkable evolution.

Chapter 10. The Challenges Ahead: Roadblocks and Mitigation Strategies

Navigating the landscape of the fashion tech industry, it's evident that it remains an expanse scattered with both opportunities and challenges. Although technological advancements have imbued the sector with unimaginable potential, an array of roadblocks and impediments stand in the way of seamless innovation and progress. This chapter aims to lay bare the multifarious challenges confronting the fashion tech industry and provide insights into strategic mitigation measures.

10.1. Obstacle One: The High Costs of Innovation

The fusion of fashion and technology is undeniably a fertile ground, rich with possibilities. However, it is also a realm characterized by high operational and developmental costs. From the initial conceptualization stages to actual product development and manufacturing, expenses can mount at an unprecedented rate.

Funding the research and development of novel materials and technologies requires considerable investment. In addition, the complexity of integrating technology into wearable fabrics necessitates specialized skills which can also significantly drive up costs. Lastly, the nature of cutting-edge, high fashion, and tech-forward design often necessitates small scale, artisanal production which does not lend itself to economies of scale, further spiking costs.

10.2. Tackling the Cost Dilemma: Investment and Collaboration

Although controlling costs in such an intricate industry may seem an uphill task, it's not an insurmountable challenge. Fashion tech firms can look to boutique investment firms or venture capitalists who specialize in early-stage tech or fashion startups. Crowdfunding platforms may also serve as an unconventional yet effective way to source funding.

Collaboration is another powerful tool. By working together with tech companies, universities or research institutions, fashion tech businesses can share the burdens of research and development. This could lead to mutual skill exchange, shared knowledge, and combined forces towards technological breakthroughs.

10.3. Obstacle Two: Consumer Acceptance and Utility

Fashion tech stands at the intersection of utility and aesthetic, sometimes swinging more to one side than the other. Products, no matter how innovative, might face consumer resistance if they do not strike a balance between utility, wearability, and aesthetic appeal. Moreover, the introduction of technology into clothing or accessories must justify itself, or consumers may see it as a mere novelty rather than something of value or need.

10.4. Fostering Consumer Acceptance: Testing and Market Research

Fashion tech firms must emphasize an iterative process that makes use of consumer feedback at every stage, right from ideation to final production. Frequent prototype testing can ensure nimble evolutions based on market demand. Additionally, market research can drastically help in understanding target demographics, their needs, their fashion preferences, and their level of tech-savviness.

10.5. Obstacle Three: Legal and Ethical Challenges

The fusion of fashion and tech also ushers in a minefield of legal and ethical issues. Intellectual property protection, data privacy issues linked to connected wearables, the use of ethically sourced and sustainable materials, and labor rights in the production chain are just a few loops in this complex maze.

10.6. Navigating Legal and Ethical Challenges: Responsible Business Practices

To tackle these challenges, companies must prioritize ethical business practices. This includes clear transparency in supply chains, focusing on sustainable sourcing and manufacturing, and ensuring strict compliance with data protection laws. Firms must be proactive in patenting their technologies and designs to protect their intellectual property rights.

All these challenges, while formidable, are far from impossible to overcome. Embarking on the fashion tech journey involves braving these obstacles, but with insight, strategy, and perseverance, they can be navigated successfully. By focusing on collaborative innovation, responsive iteration, and responsible practices, the very future of fashion tech can be molded in ways that surpass current limitations, pushing the frontier ever further. Indeed, this journey, met with resilience and innovative thinking, will shape not just the future of fashion, but the colossal role that technology will play in it.

Chapter 11. The Future: Predictions and Pathways in Fashion Tech Landscape

As we traverse this winding narrative of exploration, ingenuity, and advancement in fashion technology, it is imperative to cast our gaze towards the horizon of possibilities looming ahead of us. It is within this final segment of our journey that we extrapolate upon the developments and trends foreseen within the landscape of fashion tech, and assess the potential pathways that could carve the future of this fusion between style and technology.

11.1. The Dawning Age of Smart Clothing

Looking at the future of fashion technology, it isn't far-fetched to envision a time where clothing isn't simply a statement of style, but also an interweaved layer of intelligent hardware. This belief is born from a trend that is slowly but surely gaining momentum, backed by powerhouse designers, innovative startups and, crucially, a receptive consumer base.

The 'smart clothing' we refer to paints a picture far detached from earlier generation wearables like fitness trackers or smartwatches. Imagine garments woven with micro-sensors, able to monitor your biometrics and provide real-time feedback to your gadgets, all the while being as comfortable and stylish as your favorite outfit. From conductive fabrics to health-monitoring innerwear, breakthroughs in material science and digital technology promise an imminent convergence of fashion and tech like never before.

Although remote from mainstream adoption, an inkling of this future is already visible today, as tech giants and fashion powerhouses collaborate to develop garments that marry style with smart functionality. Conductive threads that channel electricity, clothes that work with augmented reality – the prototypes are endless and signify that the dawn of smart clothing is not a question of 'if', but 'when'.

11.2. Sustainability and Circular Fashion

The momentum building around sustainability and circular fashion is stronger than ever and plays a leading role in shaping the future of fashion tech. The growing scrutiny on the ecological implications of the fashion industry – a significant global polluter – compels brands to marry style with ethical manufacturing and sustainable practices.

The 'make, use, dispose' linear model that dominated the 20th-century fashion ethos is being replaced by concepts like 'reduce, reuse, recycle'. Advances in textile engineering have resulted in fabrics derived from seaweed, milk protein, even fermented bacteria that not only offer fascinating texture and aesthetic possibilities but also promise minimal environmental impact.

Further glimpses of this sustainable future include 3D-printed clothes that reduce manufacturing waste, clothes dyed using digital printing methods to save water and substances like Algae sequins that promise the razzle-dazzle without the environmental cost. Given the pressing need for change, it can be safely predicted that sustainability through technology would remain a cornerstone of future fashion tech development.

11.3. The Influence of Artificial Intelligence

Artificial Intelligence (AI) is expected to be the crucial driving force behind many key transformations in the fashion industry. Its applications, already visible today, range from predictive analytics for trend forecasting to personalized style recommendations for consumers on virtual platforms. The integration of AI in fashion tech could redefine personal style, brand marketing, and the retail experience on the whole.

The future of AI in fashion follows an innovative trajectory. Imagine virtual avatars that mimic your body shape and personal style, allowing you to experiment with outfits in a virtual try-on room or AI-powered algorithms that can design an entire clothing line based on popular trends and aesthetics. AI might also intervene in addressing the fashion industry's notorious inefficiencies, by optimizing production and distribution, and managing brand-consumer engagement in a more personalized and sustainable approach.

These AI-powered disruptions are not mere abstractions but rather foreseeable possibilities as we progress further into the era of fashion tech, considering the advancements showcased by brands today and the soaring investments in AI-powered solutions.

11.4. The Road of Challenges Ahead

Even with the promise of a fashion-tech revolution, significant challenges must be addressed to actualize this future. Data privacy concerns due to the increased intertwinement of personal style and digital technology is a key issue. Who owns the data that your smart clothes collect? How secure is it from cyber threats? As we embed more of our lives in technology, the line between the personal and the digital blurs, and this poses serious considerations for tomorrow's fashion tech stakeholders.

Another concern is the ensuring of sustainable practices at every phase of the tech-fashion lifecycle, from ideation to customer-life-cycle management. Eco-consciousness mustn't end at creating recyclable garments; then it extends to responsible sourcing, ethical production and bringing consumers onboard the sustainability bandwagon. As enticing as the fusion of fashion and technology may seem, its social, environmental, and ethical implications have to be examined diligently.

In conclusion, the future of fashion tech is an intriguing panorama of possibilities framed by smart clothing, sustainable practices, and AI-powered innovations, albeit one that is dotted with challenges. Forging a future that harmonizes style, technology, ethics, and sustainability is no mean feat, and how the industry navigates these exciting yet complex dynamics will shape the fashion tech story's next chapters. As we turn the page on this current chapter, eager anticipation and inspired innovation are the signposts that mark our path ahead.

www.ingramcontent.com/pod-product-compliance
Lightning Source LLC
Chambersburg PA
CBHW070140230526
45472CB00004B/1614